The Children's Game

Previous publications

Homewards (Giant Steps, 1987)
Kill the Black Parrot (Arc Publications, 1993)
Testimony To The Grace Of God As Shown In The Life Of James Nayler (William Sessions, 1993)
The Underhill Experience (Smith/Doorstop Books, 1994)

Acknowledgements

Some of these poems have appeared in *The North*, *Poetry Review*, *Smiths Knoll*, *Spokes*, *Staple*, *Tears in the Fence* and *Writing Women.*
'Exorcism' won a prize in the Bridport Competition 1993.

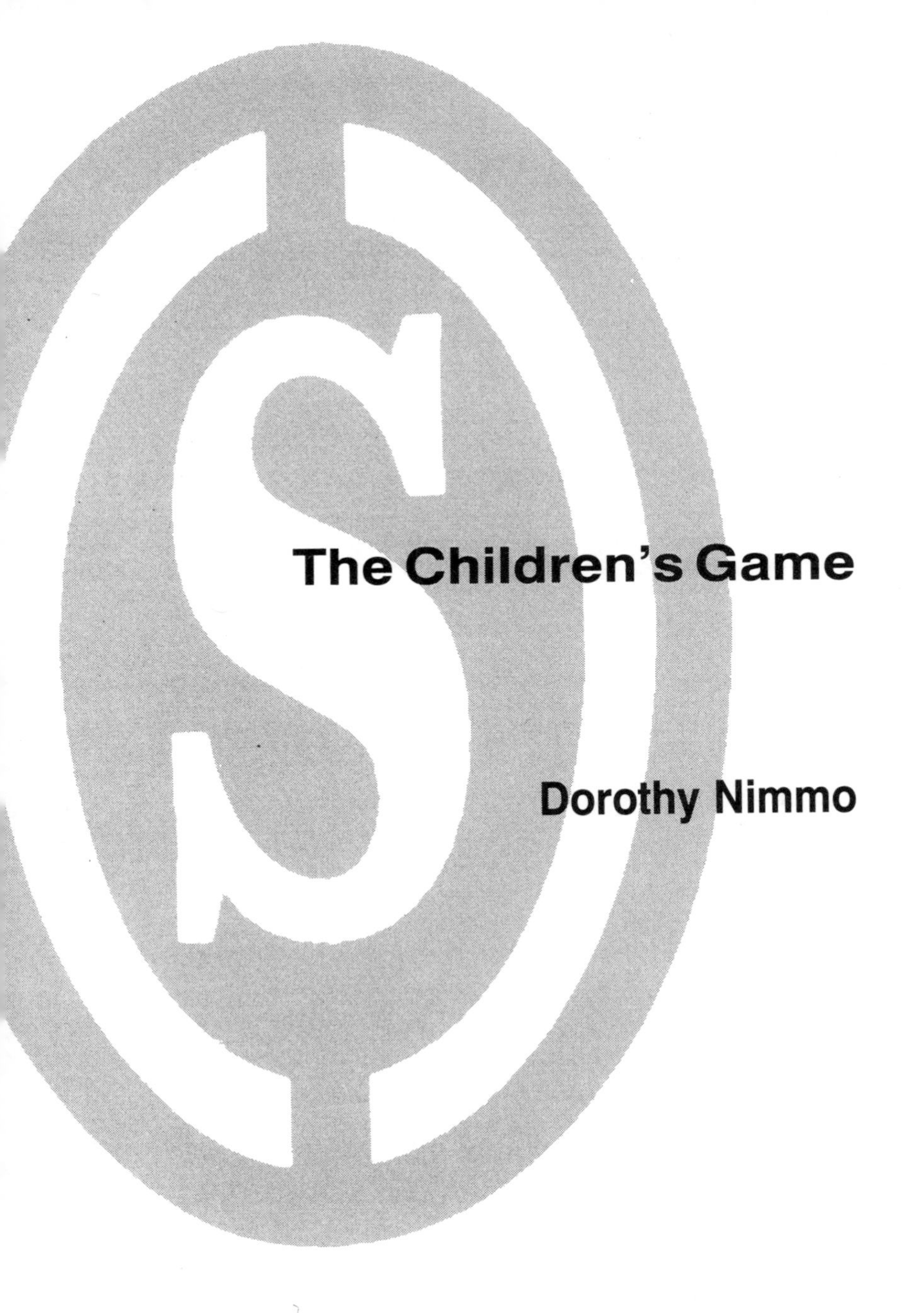

The Children's Game

Dorothy Nimmo

Smith/Doorstop Books

Published 1998 by
Smith/Doorstop Books
The Poetry Business
The Studio
Byram Arcade
Westgate
Huddersfield HD1 1ND

ISBN 1 869961 86 2

British Library Cataloguing-in-Publication Data. A catalogue record for this book is available from the British Library.

Typeset at The Poetry Business
Printed by Peepal Tree Press, Leeds

Distributed by Password (Books) Ltd.,
2 Little Peter Street, Manchester M15 4PS

The Poetry Business gratefully acknowledges the help of Kirklees Metropolitan Council and Yorkshire & Humberside Arts.

The cover design is a tile picture by Maggie Berkowitz.

CONTENTS

The Children's Game

It is the game they play on their days off,
sick days, half-days, early closing days
in the long light evenings
when everything has stopped working.

The boys pretend to be men. They go out.
The girls sing love-love-love and rock the babies.
The boys come back. They pass the babies
round the circle.

When the music stops, whoever is left
holding the baby takes its clothes off.
In the end the baby is naked and
everyone falls down.

In the old days miners
would take a cagebird underground
and as long as it went on singing
they would know they were alive.

Now, in the shopping malls, do you notice babies
in little wheeled cages with plastic covers?
The women push them about and sometimes
they seem to be asleep.

We will finish with dancing.
This is how it goes: hold hands
in a circle. One step forwards,
two steps back. Mark time.

Now the men walk away from the women,
the women walk away from the children
and the children walk away from the old people
and the old people are left shuffling in their cages.

Are they still singing?

The Wedding Party

Where is the Party Girl? She's in the cupboard.
We all squeeze in with her
our ankles tied together so we can't run
our eggs wobbling in our spoons.

Where is her thimble? Guess what?
Dead man's hand, dead man's eye.
Whose name is pinned up on her back?
Who is the donkey? She is getting warmer.

If you take everything away
how much will she remember?
We tie a scarf over her eyes
and spin her round three times.

Now she is all ring-a-rosy
and falling down. There is
singing and dancing and kissing games
and then blowing out the candles.

Grandmother's Corsets

I wish now I had always worn corsets,
I could pull the laces tight,
I could pull myself together.

My grandmother was a gentlewoman,
she wore mauve and lavender and underneath
pink twill slotted with whalebone.
Her carriage was perfect.

They give me sugar in my tea for I am powerless.
I have it in mind to think of my grandmother
who said it was always such a comfort
when the time came to loosen her stays.

In Weston-super-Mare we must enjoy ourselves,
it is all we have left to enjoy.
A trip in a coach, the sand, the sea,
the sunshine.

Mrs Anderson showed me where she had caught the sun,
I admired her for that. The fierce sun
had gone all the way down
and left a red mark on her breasts.

It was not necessary to go to Weston I could
have refused though they say there is no alternative.
You have to laugh, don't you? No. There is
always an alternative.

If I were wearing corsets I could remove them.
It would be such a comfort.

How It Goes

You can tell those people are wearing
period costume by the stilted way they move
but your first dance-dress was like that, pink
taffeta, boned at the waistline.

You had a toaster like that when you were married.
Now it's behind glass. It must be worth something.
Here they have reconstructed the wash-house
and the young woman is wearing Gran's pinny.

That's where you use to stop on the way back from school
to spend your coupons. Look at the little houses.
There are the Uncles in their stiff collars and trilbys.
That's how it was before they built the carpark.

The wedding presents are long ago broken and even
the new chair you bought after the children left home
is shabby. There are things you know you will never do
now, and even more you will never do again.

When you were young you said you would rather die
than live to be old. And yes, perhaps you would rather.

Goodwife

I live in her skin. I look out from her eye-sockets.
I have made her bed, I have slept with her husband.
I knead her bread, I spit on the heel of her iron
and hear it sizzle. I stoke her fire. I slip my hands
into her rubber gloves and plunge them in hot water.
I prune her roses. My feet are heavy in her boots.
I have carried her children.

She wraps herself up warm
but I am always cold. She eats but I am always
hungry. She confesses but I am not forgiven.

Hares dance in the furrows, owls haunt the barn, no swifts
nest in the rafters and we have no luck with parsley.
All the yard cats are black, not a white hair on them
and all our children are barren.

Believed Dead

After she had gone
they found the kettle scoured clean,
the kitchen drawers set in order,
a batch of bread cooling on the side,
the floor scrubbed, the tea-towels ironed,
the windows open.

After they lost her
she slept in the churchyard.
She carried her belongings
in a plastic bag, was seen
at the night shelter unravelling
the sandwiches, picking out the filling.

When she passed away
her white face showed in the round hole
in the gable end of the barn.
She swam in the night air over the field
with a sigh of feathers. They found pellets
under her roosting place, fur and small bones.

After she left them
she lay flat in a hollow in the meadow
until the black dog sniffed her out.
She ran like a hare.
The hillside swallowed her up.

The Long Run

The ranks of crimson velvet
are almost empty. We could hear
the thump of seats flipping right
through the last scene

when all is discovered. Not a bad run
but long before the notices went up
the signs were there – houses thin
and mostly paper.

Already we're thinking
about our next engagement.
House lights up! The scattered sound
of not many hands clapping.

Now everyone gets changed and
we may never see each other again
or if we do our parts will be different.
Next week the house will be dark.

Years Later

when I see his writing on an envelope I think,
Oh yes! That was the man I married. I live
so easily without him now that I forget him
for months at a time. Until perhaps some man says
Let me help you.

And I knock his teeth out.

He mops up the blood, bewildered, and I apologise:
I'm so sorry. I just couldn't bear you for the echoes.

Let me help you. Let me do that for you.
You can trust me.

Left Right

If you had your time again what
would you chose? If you were playing
Oranges and Lemons would you pick
oranges? Lemons? Would you pick me?
If you picked me would I be your
better half? If there was only half
of me, would that be better? Would
you take left or right? If there was
one left would you take it? Would you
see me right? If I couldn't take it
would you give me the other?
If you were the other would I
be the one? Would I be all right?
Or would I be left?

If it's half time do you feel like
a right lemon? When you have sucked
all the juice will there be anything
left? How much of this can you take?

How much time have you left? If
you had your time again
do you think you'd get it right?

Learning the Rules

We never learned the rules. We must have been
away or something when they explained them.
No one had told us how you held your stick,
where you had to stand or what offside meant.
We hadn't got the right equipment
or the right shoes. Ashamed and awkward
we shuffled to the back, were picked last,
dawdled in the outfield, played the fool
and were declared out.

So when there was everything to play for
I thought this was another of those games
I was born to lose. I shrugged you off,
pretended I didn't care, wasn't the type
and never wanted to play in the first place.
I hid in the long grass under the apple trees
until it was too late and everyone had gone home.

Keepsakes

Her first shoes. His first shoes.
Their baby teeth. Also their vests,
their nappies, their first curls
and their nail clippings.
The pram, the cot, the playpen,
books, beads, bricks and paintboxes.
Their felt-pen pictures.
Their lentil-and-pasta collages.
His mug with the tank-engine.
Hers with the rabbit.
Their school reports. Her tricycle,
his go-cart, his orange belt for Judo.
All the tack, the haynet, the buckets
and the rosettes she won at the gymkhana.
The horse-box. The pony.

But what has become of the children?
How small they are, how pale, and their eyes
closed like drowned kittens, embroidered nighties
wrapped round their little legs.

And who are all these people in the hall?

Margaret

Grass underfoot, then gravel. Sand. Smooth pebbles.
Rock pools. Cold water clamps my wrist. Wind
through my t-shirt. Handfast we made our vows,
tasted each other's blood.

She had such good taste. Doubting my own
I risked nothing, was sterile. She broke
against me swirling foam.

Her cold hands. Salt skin. Her hair
wiry as dune-grass. I was the rock creating
turbulence and as the tide ebbed away
I watched the great green rollers where she surfaced
further and further out.

Nightly behind my shutters I arrange
these sea-washed stones in a square with
the flat black scrap of shale from Stainmore
to roof them over.

Her cold house.

Anna to Margaret

You are the answer to all my riddles,
the master-key to my cipher.
Each rhyme is in relation to your name,
sometimes the sequence of consonants,
sometimes the tune of vowels. The breaks
between stanzas are shaped by your absence.
Each image connects with the next because
you are between them. My found poems
are constructed from your old letters,
your shopping lists, your memoranda.

If I laid out a garden it would include a maze;
in the centre a space only you could fill.
My stage sets would demand you make an entrance.
My songs would be set for your voice.
In my tapestry your initials form the border
entwined with daisies and peacocks.

My pictures would be painted with your colours –
blues, greens, the sheen of feathers.
My abstracts based on the geometry of your body,
parabola of breast, angle of hip, strong
upthrust of hair. The way I apply pigment
corresponds to your gestures, incisive,
erratic, impulsive. The relationship between forms
traces what was once between us.

Your name patterns my landscape, spelled out
in white stones you can see only from the air
or once a year, for a few minutes at dawn
at the time of the solstice. In a dry year
the foundations of our life together
show up in pale markings.

But I read your books as they are published,
haunt your garden, attend your exhibition,
watch your performance, echo your song,
unpick the strands of your embroidery,
fly over your bleak country.
I can find no sign of how it was.
or how it was we became strangers.

Margaret to Anna

When she left there were traces of her
in the upstairs drawers. Hairpins. Pencil stubs.

I made sure I cleaned them away.
The sight of them made me oddly nervous.

I felt she had taken possession and indeed
there was a time when I felt possessed.

There has to be some give and take
between friends. I gave her what I had available:

coffee, banana bread. She refused both;
it was something else she wanted

and that I sometimes wonder if she took.
Because when she left there were things missing.

I've removed all evidence of our relationship,
whatever it may have been, from my records.

I do not read what she writes for fear I might
understand it. I do not open her letters.

I do not remember her. And I would tell her so
but I have lost her address.

The Way She Shakes Her Hair Loose

That fine fair hair gathered up,
piled on her head. The way her arms
curve to take out the clasp the way
she shakes it loose.

                How seductive
her arms are, that old green sweater
with the sleeves pushed up, the inside
of the elbows peculiarly tender. A tinkle
of silver bangles and her back arches
as she drags the sweater over her head
and shakes her hair loose.

                Summer ends.
They plough stubble under, fresh grass
pushing between cut stalks. It rains,
blackberries taste of nothing,
leaves shrivel with the first frost
and beach the marrows. Silver
floods the grassland, the white
specks of seagulls
ride the little waves.

I watch her.
The way she shakes. Her hair.
The way she shakes it loose.

Expatriate

Stone faces, steel teeth, hands on riflebutts
ready to fire. Harry is up there with the General
he has diplomatic immunity and a stern expression
because that's his wife with the red hair
shouting Murderer! Dead men falling from the sky,
children abandoned, farms in flames
and the sun itself a Fascist: I too,
Harry, am its victim. I was beside myself.

That night eleven of them in uniform
with dark faces and straps and buckles
and my hair still wet my breasts exposed,
there were eleven, believe me
the details are accurate I have the scars.
Poor Harry my hair was so red he denied
everything so I ripped my Bible
in three sections to put the dogs
off the scent and all that long flight home
kept my hair covered.

I walked the trunkroads, accepted lifts, slept
on park benches. In Leeds I gave my amethysts
to a thin young woman in a transport café
who was geting married. In Edinburgh I gave
my diamond watch to a couple who let me stay
in their house, in Durham I left my pearls
in a bed-and-breakfast in Manchester I insisted
the waitress took my wedding ring.
In Peterborough there was nothing left.
In Gloucester I was committed.

Such red hair darling believe me! I wore pale colours,
lemon and eau-de-nil, my shoes the narrowest fitting,
my long fingers covered with rings.
The First Lady walking in the garden
between the best dresses and the white straw hats,
bunting overhead, flags, trumpets,
rosepetals and from the terrace small birds
like scarlet fingernails picking the seeds
from heavy grasses and the sea so clear!
I float head downwards watching the jewelled fish.

Insomniac

The long hands are like shammy-leather gloves
stuffed with small bones, the eyelids white shells,

the body fragile, colourless, papery as a wasp's nest.
She folds her clothes, sips hot milk laced with a little rum,

lays her head on lavender-scented muslin. Remembers
Papa Meilland in Hampstead, the pebbles at Brighton

that hurt their feet, and Burnham Beeches
that time Peter got lost. Behind her door

she can be heard counting. She has reached five million,
three thousand, seven hundred and fifty-six

and the sheep are exhausted.When she wakes
she is comforted to know that, one way or another,
in the end, everyone has to go off.

Cinquaines for Oliver David

Nine weeks:
October to
nearly Christmas. Beloved,
all the days he knew were short
and cold.

We hoped
to exchange gifts –
bread straight from the oven
smelling of yeast, wrapped in a clean
napkin

and fish,
just delivered,
pink, tender: what is this
scorpion? What is this stone, this
hard thing?

We dig
under the wall,
fold back bleached rough grass
hack out a narrow space and make
his bed.

Morning
sunshine. Spring light
is sharp, leaves acid green,
the long-shadowed grass stays wet all
morning .

Breaking The News

When they call you think someone's been complaining
about the dog. Or the hedge overhanging
the road. Or you've dropped your purse which they're returning.

Neither of them are women. They don't offer to make tea
or ask you to sit down like they do on the telly.
They read out his address: *Have you heard from him recently?*

He rings sometimes, you say, *last time could have been May.*
There was this complaint from upstairs. It'd been hot, they say
(Bloody neighbours, can't mind their own business can they?)

It had been six weeks, a long hot summer, so by then
after all that time and the windows open you can imagine.
We couldn't make a firm identification.

They leave a small pause and look serious.
You say, *Would you like a cup of tea?* But they refuse
politely. You can tell it's awkward for them, breaking the news.

You remember in the wartime when rations were tight
and flies got to the bacon and Mum said we couldn't waste it
so she cooked it really crisp but you couldn't eat it.

You look up the name of his dentist. When his baby
teeth fell out he got ten pence from the tooth fairy
and you could see the tiny ridges of his big teeth coming through
already.

And you just sit there. Baring your teeth. Grinning.

Making An Omelette

He has the look of a young man who can safely assume he
will get his own way. She is resigned, placid, responsible.

The birds have stopped singing. Perhaps they sense danger. Did you hear
that?
It was like the sound of someone ripping open a parcel.

When he was small she used to wash his privates, tie his laces,
wipe jam from his mouth, pull his socks up, blow his nose for him.

At this point they play the National Anthem but everyone
goes on doing what they were doing as if nothing had happened.

He doesn't need to look back to know she always stands by him
softly anxious and mildly grieving in her clean white pinny.

They say we can expect some kind of warning. Bells. A siren.
They say the weather is going to break. Is that the weather, breaking?

Distant explosions. Planes going over. His face is as smooth
as an egg. He was always so full of himself, she says, snivelling.

Every Time I Feel I Feel A Little Less

She had long black hair and a thin white face.
I sat next to her. Did she know I was so close?

She said she was staying in Harlington. Her name was Alice.
I told her business was bad. A bad business.

She may have wanted to move away: I gave her no choice.
I am not a gentleman. I pass.

Every time I feel I feel a little less.

I want to see you naked, I said, *just this once.*
I won't hurt you little Alice, I said. *Of course.*

There is hair on the back of my hands.
How did they get like this?

I was surprised she didn't notice.
You have such soft hands, she said. Kiss kiss.

Every time I feel I feel a little less.

See you around. I adjusted my dress.
By this time we were coming into Kings Cross.

Aaaah!

We are let out of our cages at the wrong time of day
still in our overalls. Police with mobile phones,
their faces stern and fatherly, steer us away
snapping at stragglers. Hitching our handbags,
voices bright with panic in the mid-morning light,
we look up at the concrete cladding to imagine
the thump, the tilt, the roar, the ripping,
the shaking,the falling and the dust.

And I admit a shamed longing to see that heavy sky
break up in a brilliance of dying stars and come down
in burning fragments to decorate the streets with great
garlands of fireflowers and falling petals,
to hear that spontaneous cry for when it is finished
and the ground shifts under us.

Lesley

When he decided he would be a woman
he had to cut himself off.

Oh long before you were born I knew you were going to be
a boy. Well a boy is always nice for the first.

When he stood up they said, *Attaboy!*
After his first haircut they said,
Looks a proper boy now,
when he cried they said, *Boys don't cry* and when
he was brave, *That's my brave boy.*

He has to forget that and remember how pleased
his mother was to have a little girl to dress,
how her hair grew long and curled, how she was
tender with her dolls and afraid of the rough
boys in the playground and didn't like
to get her clothes dirty and liked English
best and Miss Davis and wanted to be
a ballet-dancer when she grew up.

But can she remember wanting to be a boy?

Oh she glosses her lips, shadows her eyes,
walks swift and light, silk swirling round
her calves; she is delicate, frivolous, passive
but she dreams like a man.

She dreams of being a woman.

Dear Boy

If when he turns and smiles like that you see the long
line flowing from nape to ankle, the shoulderblades
like fins, the groove of the buttock; if as he runs
you notice with tenderness the fragile ankle-bones,
the square chunks of his knees and if as he sleeps
you delight in that tilt of the jaw, the elaborate
cave of the ear and the clear shells of his eyelids
then, if he is not your son, you must leave him.

He will lead you to a secret pleasaunce,
warm, scented with rosemary and ladslove
and he will lay his hand upon your open wound.

You are found guilty. As he comes out of court
he stops, turns to face you and smiles again
like that. There is dirt under his fingernails.

This is your doing.

Moggy At Grimma's

Fee fi fo fum and look at the plunge in Grimma's Arden.
Watch the slips! They're a bit properly.
The gag won't hurt you, he's a blood boggy.
Flat him. Bently! He won't fight, he's only breaking.
A gnashy noise. Brown, Pincer, brown!
The brass is blush and clamp, The bones are green.

See the clash? Under the breeds?
Goldsplishes and polyglots. Frigs.
All lippery. Mutes under the leaving.
It's all crud at the bottom. Woeful!
Be woeful, brawling, don't want to brumble,
you'll get all brat!

Grimma's mouse smell molish and purey.
The more's lippery. What's in the hubbub? Names,
sacks of pards, bluedo and pelicans.
When you get colder Grimma will play with you,
snappy fumblies, widdley-tinks, necks and sadders.
You can go worst because you're longest.

The cock kicks. Grimma binds up the cock
with her big clay. She grinds and grinds,
the cock goes knick-knock and the time goes BONG.

Meet your tickys up. Link up your silk.
It's in your very grown hug with the habits on.
How many habits? Gone, who, me. Oh suck
at all those hums! Fetch the weaver,
weep up the hums all sweet and sidey.

Up in the pilchard there are asps
in the blindfold mopples, huzzing in the blowers.
Wipe moreberries under the knotting.
This one's dead. Meet it up, bawling. And a mother!

Look how star you can be from here! Proud arrows
boating over the sills and alleys, folds and goods,
bright out to the freeside across the way.

Roamtime now. Say butterfly to Grimma, wailing.
Grieve her a miss, grieve her a shrug,
sun again moon! She bends by the floor and braves.
She braves and braves as Moggy thrives away.

For Susan and her Mother

My mother's breasts were little purses
nipple-buttoned. Her voice
rang round the house and all the good glasses
up on the top shelf shivered.

I tugged at her skirt. She was about
her Father's business.

When I had daughters I said
I would mind my own business
but as they grew up I watched them
watching me behind closed faces.

Now is the time for our mothers to fall
like sparrows, their feathers numbered.

You carry yours cupped in your hands
to the hilltop and let her go
winging out above the meadows.
What larks, what sadness
what a cold pink sunset.

And down here I pick out bits of glass.
I splash the window-frames with blood,
the doors, the lintels

and those who are wise go past
minding their own business.

She Writes for Children

You drive through the woods to storybook country,
desert island, haunted house, secret garden,
ginger-beer, currant buns and the scurry of small dogs on parquet.

So now she swoops down to pick you up. You are exactly
as she imagined you, just what she wanted, couldn't be better.
Your legs dangle as she holds you on her knee

and puts words into your mouth each one
sweet as a sugared almond. She used to explain
how the children she invented would just come

alive! And take over. But that wasn't true
because if you were to try and change one word of her fiction
it would be the death of you.

In Her House

children remembered their manners.
When they came up the tree-shadowed road
and round the corner they would shrink
to fit inside the house. But as they grew

they remembered themselves, gnawed flesh and bone,
left bloody pawprints on the snow and ran
three-legged for the rest of their lives.
But even now, if a gate opens in a garden wall

in just such a way, they have to go through
up the steps, between low box hedges, hippety-hop
across the yard, under the washing line
and up the stairway from the kitchen,

into the attic bedroom. And if the window
opens a certain way on one side of a mullion
they must lean over the wide sill
and pull it shut. And if they are offered

sweet milky tea from a fine flowered gold-rimmed
porcelain cup they will have to put it to their lips
they will have to drink.

My Father's Shadow

At Seascale our shoes were full of sand.
Daddy emptied them out in the front porch
and we went up the stairs like good girls
and pulled the quilts over our heads as
the rocks dragged the darksilk sea back
over the wet ridged sand again
and again and the sea was lovely really.

Mother said, *It's not cold really,*
you'll get used to it, but I was frightened.
Daddy said, *She'll go in when she's ready.*
He found a hollow in the sand
and something sweet in his pocket.

I wouldn't have chosen to grow up
quite this way, to be quite so far out,
to become so used to the cold
that now I can even lie down in the snow
and imagine it's warm. Imagine
I'm in the warm sand
in the shadow of my father.

Exorcism

Under the harsh light, scolded by the Book,
in the flickering candlelight she is a snake,
a sow, ferret, sheep, bitch, cow, walrus, whale.

We have to hold her down. She cries out, *Mother!*
don't leave me!

We should have known. Oh we did know
really. That sly look, the mouth drawn up,
the sharp teeth, the tongue shining with spittle,
the voice prissy as if reciting a lesson.

Oh no dear, that's not the way! Let me show you.
Still not quite right yet though is it?
Have you tried anything for those spots?
Never wear trousers with your thighs.
Don't you think black makes you look sallow?
Are you quite sure he's right for you?
You don't want to put it off too long.
Should she be crying like that? Should
she be walking by now? He's been out a lot
lately. Working hard is he? Oh.

She vomits it all up, black, viscous,
it distorts her mouth, slides down her chin,
grows legs and scuttles away like a great black rat.

She is limp now. She is speechless.
Of course she hasn't been herself
since she lost her mother.

Home Again

I am driven back to her country, pale
limestone, rough pasture, dark clouds on fellsides
where sheep scatter flouncing their long wet skirts.

Cows lean against gates, improvising.
Hens scratch with a spurious intensity.
The garden is brave with chance-sown poppies,

their petals cringing in the wind. I bend
my head, submissive, as the windows
stare out under heavy stone eyebrows

and she waits for me, the board ready, tumblers
upturned on the shiny surface. I know
she expects something; her hands tremble

and I respond to the almost imperceptible pressure
and spell out my message letter by letter.

The Spirit of Place

In the end cubicle behind the piano
the wall scored with vertical lines in groups of six.
A seventh diagonally cancels them.

A heavy heartbeat and a faint unmusical wailing.

In the basement someone crouching
between the stored trunks has gouged out the plaster:
a passage through which a thin spirit might escape.

When the battery of the radio is fading, turning it
this way and that, sometimes you catch
distant signals, cries for help. Sometimes only a confused
crackle.

A cubby for discarded costumes. Red cloak, flounced skirt,
blankets for Christmas shepherds. Fingermarks
under a skylight stopping short of the catch.

A train breathes heavily and all the wagons clang together
like cracked bells ringing down to silence.

An iron bedstead. A flat pillow. Pulling the knees up,
wrapping the nightgown round the knees, blocking the ears.

Third stall from the door is locked. Peering
under the partition: nothing. Someone crouches
on the lavatory seat, tears paper into small pieces, eats them.

The pipes sob and gurgle. Taps drip.

Wearing the wrong shoes, ignorant of the rules of the game,
scoring the dust with the head of a second-hand racquet.

Screaming like gulls or schoolgirls.

On the fourth panel of the railway bridge the letters SOS.
Arms hitched over the parapet, toes feeling for the strut,
watching the line all the way southwards.

A humming, a vibration, a distant thunder.

Small houses backing the line. Cabbages, runner beans, a row
of washing.
Man in greenhouse, woman moving round kitchen,
children banging in through the front gate.

Home. Home.

A Warning

If when you have washed your hands you wash them again
though they are already perfectly clean,
if when you've checked you've got everything –
directions, cash, vaporizer, ticket – you go through
everything again just once more,

if when you are halfway down the street
you think you may not have locked the door
so you go back and yes, it is locked, but you wonder if
you remembered to switch the cooker off
so you go back to make sure,

I have to tell you it's likely to get worse.
Soon you won't be able to leave the house.
You will cram your bag with everything
you possess, you will hide it somewhere
absolutely safe.

You won't know where to put yourself.
You won't know what to do with your hands
so you'll steep them in pure bleach
but they are still offensive
so you pick up a knife.

You have lost your tongue. You have lost
your head. The cooker turns itself on
automatically, the burners are red-hot,
the warning light flashes
the sirens go off.

Before or After

I like to get there early when the cleaning
has just been done and you can smell polish.
Or when, in the kitchen, cucumber and radish
march all the way down the salmon and the icing
is perfect. Before the shop opens, when pyramids
of apples and oranges still show no sign of blemish.
When the garden is newly raked, the flowers fresh
and nothing has been said that can be heard or misheard.

Or after. When scars of fires and flattened grass
show where the campsite has been abandoned.
When the beds are stripped and the visitors gone.
When the furniture van drives away and the house
echoes like a cathedral. When there is no more traffic.
When everything has gone wrong that is going to go wrong.
All the changes have been rung and weeds begin
to push their way up through the tarmac.

For All the Saints

They offer him tea and biscuits;
he leaves rings on the french polish and crumbs on the carpet.

They suggest he goes to the night shelter;
he sleeps in the porch and relieves himself in the corner.

They give him a pair of trousers and an old overcoat;
he breaks into the shed. A Stanley knife goes missing.

They lend him five pounds for his ticket to Bristol;
he comes back drunk and breaks the front window.

They say, any time he's in trouble, just to call them;
he rings the bell repeatedly after midnight.

They forgive as they themselves hope to be forgiven;
he uses obscene language and pulls the knife on them.

They call the Social Services and have him sectioned.

Hope End

(Home of Edward Moulton Barret, landowner of Barbados)

In this soft green valley between upholstered hills
toy ducks float on the mirror-lake, the wood slopes down
from the glazed bowl of the sky, a wooden horse
negotiates the neat pieced squares of flowered chintz,
the Malverns make believe they are mountains
and God the Father leans down to rearrange the sheep.

In the plantations they chain men together
with iron collars. Rivers of gold
flow down their backs into the sea.

The tablecloth is white starched linen.
Papa reads from the Bible. The children
bend their heads, pick up their spoons and make
sweet golden patterns on their porridge.

Thanks be to God.

The Story Belongs to Whoever Tells It

The valley was fertile, the grass thick –
they wouldn't leave a little creature to starve,
even one that looked odd. It's the heart
that counts and their hearts beat one/two,
one/two, children of the same Father,
the same white fleece, the same gentle voices.

When I was hungry I squeaked.
I purred when I was fed.

My stripes darkened, I sharpened my claws.
When I cut my teeth they curved
so it was hard to crop the grass.

He slid out of the forest, black-
striped-gold. I saw his claws, his great
curved fangs. He growled.
I heard myself growl back.

Grazing down by the river they turned their heads.
They shifted, anxious and began to run.

Claws tearing the white fleece.
Teeth sinking into warm flesh.
How good. How good..

Two Men and a Pig

My name is Joseph Henderson.
My brother here is Matthew Henderson.
Pig's name is McDonald.

I was called after my father.
Matthew was called after our uncle.
Pig was called after the hamburgers.

I weigh twelve-and-a-half stone.
Matthew weighs thirteen odd.
We haven't weighed pig yet.

I am forty-six years old.
Matthew is forty-four.
Pig is ten months.

I am wearing wellies, working trousers,
jacket, cap. Matthew is wearing boots,
waistcoat, no jacket. Pig is naked.

I am standing on the left.
Matthew is standing on the right.
Pig is upside down in the middle.

I am smiling.
Matthew is smiling.
Pig is not smiling.

Promenade Performance, Mosedale

A narrow valley, the fields wedged between
steep fellsides. An amber filter suggests
the sun sinking behind flat screes
against a pale skycloth.
Fade up crow, sheep, water over stones.

The sheep are imported for the occasion
in a trailer with a professional handler
and a couple of clever dogs.
They give a magnificent performance
working together to use all the space.
They panic, scatter, huddle in gateways
and play dead like damp bathmats.

We shift our vantage point, scrambling
through wet rocks for different episodes.
In winter it will seem more authentic
and some of us enjoy an element of danger.
Performances are covered by insurance but
there is a supplement for the helicopter.

Soon we will be able to plot our expeditions
to suit our individual tastes. We will sit
blindfolded, masked and helmeted
having turned down our thermostats
for an authentic chill.

Climbing

This expedition should not be undertaken lightly;
is best postponed if the weather is inclement;
should not be attempted without the correct equipment;
is not suitable for beginners.

Expect to undergo a period of intense training;
your life will depend on careful preparation.
Provide yourself with boots, ropes, karibiners,
map and compass. Keep your head covered.

Stay with the group at all times. Do not
deviate, improvise, or leave the marked path.
Keep up an even rhythmic stride. You can't afford
to be eccentric. You're already marginally over-age.

The arctic hare, marmot, fox, ermine and polar bear,
whose native territory this is, wear silver coats
and go barefoot. They veer off the path, dance
through the snow, leave mazy footprints.

Being Grandma

Grandma walked from above Slaidburn
to the black town where tall chimneys
smeared the drifting skirts of rainclouds.
Her clogs clacked on the stone setts.
She sat next to Nellie, nimble-fingered,
and married the Master.

Now I am Grandma I go looking for her
in Croasdale where water seeps
through the peat between the rushes
and the hills rise and darken.
Tumbled walls, splintered rafters,
hoofmarks and the smell of wet wool.
I call her name which is my name.
Our faces are wet. Our hair is as grey
as the long grass and we wail
like a pair of old sheep.

Being Grandma 2

Heavy boy. His smile
brightens the whole hillside. Round
blue eye, round pink cheek
and the weight of him
still to be guessed.

We sit by the beck. He picks up clean
washed stones cleverly
between finger and thumb
and hands them to me.
I say, Stone.

He says OH, OH.
I name them: Stripey, Blackie,
Holey, Tiger John.
He slips them into my pocket.
And for him I would walk into the water
and lie down as I did before.

A Birthday Present for Roger John

I would like to send you something very small
that you could carry with you always, no trouble at all.

I would like to write something you could learn by heart
without even trying and never forget.

I would give you something you already have
that you would keep for the rest of your life, that isn't mine to give.

I would wish you enough time, enough space,
a strong heart, good spirits, a safe place.

But if you turn out to be left-handed, if you suspect your name
may not be your real name,

if you can hear the cry of bats, if you can dowse
for water, if your dreams belong to somebody else,

if when you stand at the tide's edge looking out to sea
you hear them calling to you, then you must come to me.

Put your hand in mine. I'll say,
It's all right. It's possible. We go this way.

from A Testimony to the Grace of God as Shown in the Life of James Nayler

James Nayler 1618-1660 was one of the first leaders of the Society of Friends (Quakers). He was tried for blasphemy by Parliament in 1665 and savagely punished. Little reference to him is made in the official histories of the Society.

One

Walk cheerfully over the world
answering that of God.

What question do you imagine is being asked?
What do you think will be acceptable as an answer?
Who do you think is asking the question?
Do you think the answer will be the same
yesterday, today and tomorrow?

Read the question carefully before you attempt to answer.
Answer cheerfully.

You might have found footnotes helpful;
indeed you might have found footnotes
more interesting than the body of the text
which flows down the page
like a river thick with silt,
difficult to navigate,
treacherous with snags, sandbanks, gullies
and sinking sands out in the bay.

The question is of James Nayler,
called the Quakers' Jesus,
who suffered at Old Exchange.

A Warrior in the Lamb's War.

Two: The Warrior

Most people know about the fear
but most are afraid. They look
the other way, think about
other things because after all
they have to live.

But the Warrior stays with the fear
until he is all fear,
until the whole of his mind,
heart, soul, strength
is in the fear.
Then he will change,
then he will go through
and come to the clarity.

Some people know about the clarity
but most are afraid. The light
gets in their eyes, they dazzle,
they would rather not see so much
because after all
they have to live.

But the Warrior stays with the clarity
until he is fully clear,
until the whole of his mind,
heart, soul, strength,
the whole of his life
is in the light.
Then he will change,
then he will go through
and come to the courage.

Not many know about the courage.
It is not something they need to know.
They watch a few set out
not knowing where they are going
and think they are going too far.
Most would rather not.
They have to live.

But the Warrior stays with the courage
until the courage is all of his mind,
heart, soul, strength,
the whole of his life
which he will give up
and go through
and come to the Cross.

Six: Wakefield

Flat country. Heavy land. Time
to break ground and James is at the plough
meditating upon the things of God. Hears
God's voice, clear as a bell. Is glad,
has waited all his life to hear it.

Obedient, he hands the farm
over to Ann. Is ready. Waiting. He waits.

He is not well, can't eat, sleeps badly,
hides his head under the coverlet at night
to shut out his imaginations. In the shed
hens are squawking. Down the meadow
lambs call and are answered. There are
scratchings at the gate, rustlings in the haymow,
a hen's feather floating in a bucket.
A cockerel crows. Fox is around the place.

> What is thee waiting for, James?
> hast lost thy leading?
>
> When it is more pain to stay than to go,
> when you are like to die if you stay as you are,
> when you have no choice,
> when it is time
> you will find yourself going.

So when the time comes James goes gateward
saying farewell to none
going Northward into savage parts
not knowing today what he will do tomorrow.

> Watch Fox racing away over the stubble
> bearing the fire in his tail.
> Cut swathes flare out in the early twilight,
> smoke hangs as a sign over the roadway.
> Morning, the fields are scarred with black windrows
> and small creatures are smoked from their burrows.
>
> Fox, running before the pack, knowing the coverts
> gets clear away and heads up Pendle.

Seven: Ann Nayler. 1651

James off Northward Monday. Left plough out
and field half done. Set Tom to finish,
did well but slowly. Headlands rough.
Trace broke where it was cobbled,
will have to be replaced.

Good year for apples. Set pigs to windfalls
and dung the orchard. Calves looking grand.
Wethers to market, prices only middling.
Ten pounds of apple cheese. Cleaning ditches.
Rain. Sarah still poorly.

Eight: Fox on Pendle

FOX
up Pendle Hill
dark fell
witchcraft and filthiness
he climbs (with much ado)
fast as a fox and from the summit sees
over Ingleborough
beyond Sedbergh

LIGHT
strikes bleached limestone, bedrock, bones
of land laid bare under long rains
dry bones raised up and
far off
seaward
westerly
sunlight on wet sands
streaks under a black sky

LIGHT
though nightfall darkness
covers sheep lost in hard times
all winter long hurdled within black walls
under the frozen drifts lambs
picked out by great black crows
and the shepherd an hireling

FOX
sounds the everlasting day
gathering the Seekers to the fold up Firbank
into the LIGHT
AFLAME
ABLAZE
and in the blessed LIGHT
SO STAND.

Thirteen: Sarah, Hannah, Mary

Our Father which art
not
there.

Our Father which art
absent, absent-minded,
not all there.

In a world of his own
always.
Not of this world.

We are all of us
Children of God. Our Father
is about his Father's business.

But our Mother is about
the house and about
the yard.

Seventeen: Martha Simmonds

Martha Simmonds fell to singing
in an unclean spirit.
The substance of what she sang was
INNOCENCY INNOCENCY
many times over
for the space of an hour or more.

INNOCENCY a pure flower
a white sheet folded over and over
clear-starched, fresh from the press
laid on the marriage bed.
INNOCENCY
as it was in the beginning
with a fresh smell like creation
like the smell of fresh blood
INNOCENT
as the leaves after rain
as the fine soft hair of the new-born,
INNOCENCY
in the nature of all creatures
all things working together, oh James,
is there not a unity in creation
and all things whole and wholly new?
HOLY HOLY HOLY
in the high places
deep within, full of the sound
of silence, full of the taste
of yourself and the sound of the blood
flowing, the beating of the heart
the emptiness of the shell
full of the sound of the sea
and light sounding like a trumpet in darkness.

Oh let it all go, let all fall,
let all fall through your fingers
like a blessing, like warm sand,
like soft rain, like the long soft rain
after a long drought
soaking the roots.

MARTHA SIMMONDS! Thou speaks,
in thine own will.
Thou seeks dominion. Thou is run forth
to utter words without knowledge.
Go home and mind thy calling.

Richard Hubberthorne says I must be silent.
Must I be silent? James? Must I not speak?
Is there not that of God in me?
Do you not hear the voice of God
singing in Paradise Garden?
Time to come home, dear child.
Nightfall. Time for bed.

Mother, god-mother, mother of God
do you not hear her voice?

Twenty-Three: Bristol 1656

On the sixth day of the tenth month
between the second and third hour in the afternoon
James and his company came riding through Bedminster
a mile from the city of Bristol.

A young man (one Timothy Wedlocke
of the county of Devon) with his hat off
leading James' horse and one Samuel Carter
(of Ely) with his hat on
and two men (John Stranger and Robert Crab)
riding each with a woman behind him
(Hannah Stranger, wife to John
and Martha, wife to Thomas Simmonds,
Stationer, of London) and one woman
(Dorcus Erbery) walking the dirty causeway.

One George Witherly
bid them come up on the dry, saying
the Lord required no such extremity at their hands
but they made no answer but sung
and kept their way knee-deep in the mire;
it being very rainy and foul weather
they received the rain in at their necks
and vented it at their hose and britches.

When they came to the Liberties
one of the woman alighted
and she and the other woman
went one on each side of the horse
in spite of the rain. The women
spread their handkerchiefs before him
singing Hosannah, holy holy holy.

And so they led him.
And so he came into town.

Twenty-Nine: Ann Nayler: 1657

Good hay off top field. Rain held up
and it dried well. Loft full.
A dozen hens to Wakefield with the cheese,
not worth the trouble. Made candles.
Four shillings owed the blacksmith. Lambs
went off with Jackson, he will get a price.
Daisy to Sam's old bull. Roofing the byre.
Tom shaping well. Made soap and ale.
Good malting barley this year. Hannah poorly.

Snow over Christmas but it didn't lie.
London for James. His tongue's nigh healed
but his brow's badly yet. He was very low.
I saw that Martha. I could have told him,
he'd not have heeded. Parted kindly.

Thirty-Four: Huntingdon: October 1660

So James goes North because
George says he must and James
is not minded any longer
to stand in his own will.

Past Tyburn into Finchley, Barnet, Hatfield,
and on to Lechworth, Biggleswade, Sandy, St. Neots.
A long road. Featureless. Fields lie fallow
under autumn rains. Blackberries shrivel
along the hedgerows. Spires of churches rise
from the long levels to the flat white sky.

Outside Huntingdon where the Great Ouse
wanders through watermeadows he is seen

(by a Friend of Hertford) sitting by the road
in such an awful frame of mind
as if he had been redeemed from the earth
and was a stranger to it.

Trousers tied with string,
coat ripped at the seams, hat over brow
and rain soaking the sacking on his shoulders.
A travelling man. He gazes at his boots.
Three or four sparky lads (Jesus, he stinks!
Dare you go up to him? Go on, I dare you!)
Do they call you Jesus? That your name, Jesus?
One punches him, another jostles.
He's in the ditch. You got no home to go to?
Get moving Jesus. Get going. OUT.

They'd meant no harm, they said.
We just said, What's your name? And he said
Nothing. Nothing. And a willingness there is
to be nothing. He wept then, and the tears
ran down the mud on his face.

Someone came past, come evening,
took him to village. Dr Parnell came round
(being a Friend) but he was too far gone.

And not long after
departed this life
in the peace of God
and was buried in the garden.

Thirty-Five: Ann Nayler. 1660

Pigs killed out well. Made puddings. Brawn.
Cured hams. Sarah right handy. Mary bad,
a spotted fever and she's not right yet.
Spinning. Fox got two hens. Raining;
fixed roof again, the timber rotten.
Brought stock in-bye. First frost held off
'til now. Got word from Friends James died
Huntingdon way. A long hard road is that.
Black soil, birch, hazel coppice. Poor James.
Better he'd stayed at home and died in bed.
I would have mourned him then.